T0193609

My Devotions
and Poems
Just for You

LINDA FORTNER

WESTBOW
PRESS®
A DIVISION OF THOMAS NELSON
& ZONDERVAN

Copyright © 2018 Linda Fortner.

All rights reserved. No part of this book may be used or reproduced by any means, graphic, electronic, or mechanical, including photocopying, recording, taping or by any information storage retrieval system without the written permission of the author except in the case of brief quotations embodied in critical articles and reviews.

Scripture taken from the New King James Version®. Copyright © 1982 by Thomas Nelson. Used by permission. All rights reserved.

WestBow Press books may be ordered through booksellers or by contacting:

WestBow Press
A Division of Thomas Nelson & Zondervan
1663 Liberty Drive
Bloomington, IN 47403
www.westbowpress.com
1 (866) 928-1240

Because of the dynamic nature of the Internet, any web addresses or links contained in this book may have changed since publication and may no longer be valid. The views expressed in this work are solely those of the author and do not necessarily reflect the views of the publisher, and the publisher hereby disclaims any responsibility for them.

Any people depicted in stock imagery provided by Thinkstock are models, and such images are being used for illustrative purposes only. Certain stock imagery © Thinkstock.

ISBN: 978-1-9736-1768-6 (sc)
ISBN: 978-1-9736-1767-9 (e)

Library of Congress Control Number: 2018901250

Print information available on the last page.

WestBow Press rev. date: 04/20/2018

In memory of my mother. She was my encouragement
in all areas of life, especially my writing.

Contents

Happy Birthday

Some cousins are special,
And some are not.
But, lucky you, you fall
In the first slot.

Since you were little,
I've always been glad
To have you for a cousin,
Even when you made me mad.

You were so cute with that
Ponytail flipping around,
A cute little smile,
Seldom a frown.

I'm lucky to have you for a cousin.
You see,
You're much more like a sister
Would be to me.

Happy birthday, Terri.
This is from the heart.
Many more, dear cousin.
I hope we never drift apart.

I'm proud of you and all you do,
Being a good mother and
A grandmother too.

January 24 is a special day
'Cause you were born.
What more can I say?

Friends

Some friends are old. Some friends are new.
Some friends are more special and will
See you through.

Some friends are funny, and some are not.
Some friends need your help,
As much as you've got:

If you are short on friends as a whole,
Maybe you should be a better friend.
This much I know.

You have to be a friend to have a friend.
It is really so.
Hold your friends close to your heart.
They are worth more than gold.

Our church is the best place to meet new friends.
They are truthful and loyal.
They are there for you.
On them you can depend.

Remember each and every day
To be a good friend in every way.
The blessings you get will be your pay.

Lost a Friend

You lost a special friend today.
It's hard for me to know
What to say.

You'll miss her laugh, her silly ways.
I know you will think of her
Every day.

But try to remember
The happy times,
How special she was
To you.

She was so very funny
And had a good heart,
One of a kind
Through and through.

She would brighten the room
When she entered it.
She could light up the world
With that gigantic grin.

Be glad God gave you a friend
Like her.
We don't know why things
Like this occur.

But as she would say if she were here,
Things happen for a reason,
Even if we shed a tear.

Few people have a friend like
You two have had.
God gave you this, so don't be sad.

The memories you have will never leave.
Cherish them close.
It's okay to grieve.

Remember the good times,
And laugh at the bad.
Be glad for God's gift
Of this friend you had.

Holidays

The holidays are here again,
A time for love and cheer,
A time for all of us to share,
To show we really care.

Decorations all around and
Smiles on every face
Really make each one of us know
Tonight we're in the right place.

Let's share this time of Christmas joy,
Making memories here tonight.
Laugh and smile tonight, my friends.
Have a wonderful time with us.

Your being here completes tonight.
Your presence is a must.

Merry Christmas to each one of you.
Remember, God loves each one too.

Spread happiness to someone else.
Try not to think of just yourself.
God has blessed us this whole year through.
Try to make God proud of you.

Barron

A bundle of energy and
Smiles are his ways.
Ever since a baby,
He's loved to play.

As a boy, he was busy
Fixing and tinkering,
Changing things around,
He and Kelly bickering.

A deep love for Barron I feel
In my heart.
Even though he is tough,
He cares for others, and he's
Smart.

He goes four-wheeling and boating,
Hunting and all,
Fishing and trucking.
He seems to have a ball.

People like him, from young
To old!
I'm proud he's so funny
And well liked by all.

I'm proud of this man
Who developed from my boy.
I'm proud I'm his mother.
He has brought great joy.

In my prayers, I remember
To mention his name.
I hope he remembers me
And feels the same.

Fathers

Fathers are hard to write about.
They have so much influence
On our life's map.

They are not all perfect,
And that's a fact.
But most really try—
You have to give them that.

Fathers are to be the heads
Of their homes.
Fathers make you feel good.
Their influence is strong.

Some are stern, and some smile
All the time.
Either way, they are loved
In your heart and mine.

Thank you, God, for our
Fathers on the earth.
And thank you, God,
For our heavenly Father first.

Son

I'm very proud of you, Caleb,
And all that you are.
I just couldn't ask for a son
To be more.

You are not perfect, I know,
And I'm sure think me silly.
I can't help but be happy that you
Are so very witty.

You're polite and so smooth.
No waves do you make,
But can't be pushed too far
Or you can get mad as an ape.

I'm proud of your football and
Desire to do right.
I admire you because you
Don't look for a fight.

You have a unique way about you,
And I feel you will go far.
People will respect you.
You are a leader and
Can do what you desire.

Stay close to God. He will guide
You through.
If you have God, all the decisions
Don't have to be made by you.

I don't worry about you.
You know right from wrong.
Your will can save you.
It is very strong.

Valentine

A valentine may be big or small.
You can make it, say it, or
Buy it at the mall.

It usually says, "I love you," in a
Very witty way,
Or maybe it's romantic and
Will really make your day.

Hearts and flowers, cupids and
Arrows,
Made from satin and lace
And things of good taste.

You don't have to be twenty to
Enjoy this attention.
Don't you agree with these things
I have mentioned?

It may all sound silly, especially
To the men,
But I will tell you a secret:
It is not silly to us hens.

You don't have to earn them
In any form or fashion.
You just take them and say
Thank you with some sort
Of sweet reaction.

I hope that I get one and that
All of you do too.
I'm sure if we don't, we will all
Be in a stew.

Class of 1954

Remembering days gone by
Brings a smile to each one's face.

Fifty-four students full of life and ready
To leave this place.
A group who thought we knew
It all
Would give this world a whirl.

A close group we were as we look back,
Children, friends, and all of that.

We knew who had tempers, and we knew
Who to trust. We were
Ready for anything.
Graduation was a must.
So, in 1954 in a little country school,
Fifty-four students were ready to rule.
The memories are ones we will
Cherish forever.

We all had such a great time.
Forget it? Never.

Everyone went this way and that,
But in our hearts, we were
Close no matter where we
Were.

Some may have left us, others never
Went far,
But look around, friends.
Here we are!

Now some were smarter, and some
Not so bright.
We won't mention names 'cause some can
Still give a good fight.

In fifty years, we will all meet again.
Class of 1954 will always be friends.

Banquet of Love

A banquet of love is here for your pleasure.
We hope your enjoyment is way beyond measure.

Love is a feeling you have in your heart.
You show it, you feel it, and
You give others your part.

God's love is given to each one of you.
He expects us to pass this love on through.

If we all give love as we receive,
Then lots of people will
Receive exactly what they need.

A flower, a note, a smile
Will all help
Make someone happy and
Feel good about self.

Hopefully, we gather here tonight
Full of love
To shine for the Lord,
Who is watching from above.

Red hearts and candy are all
Very sweet.
Let us all show Christ's love
To all whom we meet.

Love one another
As our Lord loves you,
And this love
Will be passed back to you.

God will smile on Riverside Church.
He will know we have put
God's way first.

Riverside Women of Faith-2002

Women of Faith was a new
Experience for me.
Betty was at the wheel of the van,
And the events of that trip
Were great to see.

We arrived.
We were divided to our rooms.
Rushing about,
Freshened up, loaded up.
We were Women of Faith-bound.

It was awesome to see so many
Women in one spot.
*How did this many women
Get away?* is what I thought.

Can you imagine the vision?
Big screens, so big you did
Not miss one thing,
Every expression on each
Person as they spoke or sang.

We sang, we prayed, tears
Flowed, and we laughed.
It was a sharing that I'll cherish
All the days I have left.

Our speakers were good.
Our music was too.
All the blessings I received
I would love to pass to you.

God gave me this time to
Know our ladies better.
I love each one with
A new way of together.

If you get a chance to ever
Go and take part,
Grab that chance—you'll
Love it with all
Your heart.

Be Thankful

Be thankful for what you have.
Stop worrying about that you
Have not.

Do you have a home and
Food on your table?
Are you breathing?
Getting up in the morning,
Are you able?

When you open your eyes,
Are you able to see?
Is there a roof over your head?
Sure, we all have needs!

Think about what you have,
About what really matters.
Don't waste your thoughts and
Worry what could have been better.

In your days of the future,
Leave your worries behind.
Let God be your focus.
Happier times you will find.

Angels

There are angels here tonight.
Look around. Can you see?
Can you guess where they sit?

Some people think angels are
All blondes with great wings.
Beautiful creatures with harps,
They all sing.

I believe angels are all shapes
And sizes.
Gray hair. Brown hair.
Looks are not really what
God emphasizes.

Have you ever felt like someone
Came from out of the blue,
Was in the right place
To help someone like you?

Maybe a sad time when you lost
Someone dear,
God sent just the right person
To bring you some cheer.

Some angels may have harps
And wings,
But others are not so radiant
And don't even sing.

Have a happy life and please
Keep in mind
Angels are among us
all the time.

A Simple Plan

It's as simple as can be,
The formula for life's quality.
If only we could all try our best.

Think of others instead of just yourself.
For a moment, leave your wants
On a shelf.

If every person tried their best
To bring a smile to someone's face,
How could we fail with the human race?

For just one day, try my simple plan—
Even if it feels a little strange, my friend.

You will see a difference in your life.
We may not cure the world in one day,
But then again, who can say?

Welcome Basket

If Lookout Valley could give you
A treat to keep in your basket this year,

You would be able to reach right inside
And have just what you wanted
In the flash of an eye.

A basket full of anything or everything you want—
To eat, to read.
You would never hear the word *no*!

Anything to drink? A piece of gum to chew?
A good book to read?
All of this, just for you!
Your stay with us would be complete.

Just reach right inside.
A fan? Some lotion?
Just anything that you have a notion.
The easy button would have nothing on us,
Because this basket is just a must.

Only special people would be given a gift such as this,
Especially people like you, if you catch my drift.

You would reach right
In for ideas and strength for each day.
A prayer, a friend,
Whatever you may.

A little bit of energy when you're feeling tired.
A nice massage for your muscles
When your day was especially hard.

You are very special to us.
We are thrilled to have you here.
So enjoy this basket.
It is full of good cheer.

Full of eastern star and a prayer for your stay.
Remember Lookout Valley
And return this way some day.

Why Worry

Why do we worry all the day long?
Why this or that happens.
What could I have done?

Sometimes we worry over what is to come—
What if this or what if that.
Have our thoughts start to

God is in charge all of the time.
Why should we worry?
He is our king,
Yours and mine.

He will see that life follows the
Flow that is to be.
Pray daily that all is his
Will for you and me.

The Bible tells us over and over again:
Look to your Lord;
He is your best friend.

When times are rough and hard to bear,
Our precious Savior is there.
He really cares.
Be consistent in prayer.
God's will to be done.
Worry no more.—hold tight to your faith.
All works for God's children.
Spread hope in this place.

Be there for your friends—
And family too.
Let God have his way
To work through you.

The kicker is this, and remember it is true:
Pray for your enemies.
God will take care of me and you.

Special Daughter

A daughter is special,
And you are the best.
You're a diamond, my dear,
In the midst of the rest.

You've given me such joy
As you've shared your
Life with me.
Thank you, dear daughter,
For being close to me.

We've shared our silly times.
You invited me to join in.
You're not only my sweet daughter
But a very good friend.

A new road now you're taking.
Remember all I've said.
Stay close to God. He'll
Pull you out when you
Think you're in quicksand.

A happy life with your husband
Awaits you now, my dear.
But remember, if you need me,
I'll always be here.

A part of me is sad
As you leave our home,
But a joy in my heart rejoices
As you create a new, happy home.

You'll always be my daughter,
Regardless of where you live.
So, smile, little one, as
A new life for you begins.

I pray one day you may have
A daughter sweet as you,
And only then will you
Remember how much
I truly love you.

Now happiness awaits you.
Oh, where did the years go?
I feel now we may even grow closer
As you start to grow.

Let's still share our silly times.
Let's still go for yogurt.
But now the difference will be
We won't take along your brothers!

Grandmother

Not many are so lucky
To have a grandmother like me.

She held a love in her heart
For her garden and flowers.
She loved horses and K-mart
And dogs of all sorts.
She meant you to come if she
Called you from her porch.

My cousins and I loved her since
We were but small.
When up at her house, we all
Had a ball.

The whole bunch would come
On Sundays for lunch.
Her happiest times were spent
When she had the entire bunch.

Family was important to her,
You see.
She thought we were special,
As special as could be.

We all learned quickly the rules
Of her game.
Stay out of her flowers,
Or you would feel pain.

She was spunky and tough and
Loving and sweet,
And now we will miss her
And hold memories sweet.

But now she is happy, and no
Pain will she bear.
For she is now with Granddaddy,
And a new place they can share.
So, we smile as we think
How happy she must be
In God's heavenly kingdom
As she waits for you and me.

Mothers and Daughters

Mothers and daughters have a special bond.
We are connected at the heart; the love goes on and on.

Sometimes we don't see eye to eye.
We argue and fight and may even cry.

But when the smoke clears, we will have that love
That is a gift, sent from above.

Some mothers are sweet, and some are kind.
Others are bossy and do not want to hear you whine.

Daughters can be special and steal your heart.
Even if they are sassy, you never want to part.

All in all, it's a wonderful role
To be a mother and daughter until you grow old.

There are a lot of mothers and daughters who are not even blood kin,
But it's all in the heart; it lies deep within.

God knew how special this bond would be.
Without our mothers, where would we be?

My Favorite Daughter

Sometimes we don't agree and seem
Like we're going to fight,
But mostly it's just because, you see,
We're so much alike.

The same beautiful smile and sweet laugh.
The same cute, round face.
And it goes on.

But, really and truly, I'm happy
As can be to have a daughter
Like you of my own.

I always wanted you to be a lot
Like me—
But lots better in more ways
Than one.

You are that for sure.
I'm so proud of you.
Look what you have done,
And life's just begun.

You're my favorite daughter.
You've already done
So much I wished you could do.

Congratulations on your nursing degree.
Good work, my dear, and
Well done.

Your Mom

My Caleb

Caleb is special.
He is one of a kind.
I am so proud to say
He is a son of mine.

From the start, he was
Special even as a babe.
What joy he has brought us.
So much he gave.

Worldwide wrestling
And Ninja Turtles were his bag.
The spy toys he needed,
His aim to play a gag.

We moved up to baseball.
He was quite a hit.
Followed his basketball
But later decided to quit.

He shaved his head.
Even though I griped,
Caleb thought it looked great.
He was out of sight.

Football now is the love
He has.
He works hard working out
And all that jazz.

Now Caleb is sixteen
And ready to drive.
Where have the years gone?

If the next sixteen years
Are as wonderful as the first.
We are all so proud of him.
I hope I don't burst.

Caleb is becoming a wonderful
Young man.
I know he'll do his best,
The best that he can.

Kelly, Barron, and Tony agree.
We're glad God gave us Caleb
For our family tree.

My Church

My church is a special place to go.
It touches my heart and
Warms my soul.

The people here are friendly and true.
They sincerely care about me
And you.

God's love is here, and his presence
Is sweet.
I feel it inside each and every week.

Lift up your hands and praise
Our Lord.
He's coming again, and oh, our hearts
Soar

As we wait for the Lord, praying
Daily for strength.
This place is so special, and what
A blessing we get.

Our altar is a most reverent place
To kneel and confess and ask God
For his grace.

It's okay here to shed a tear or lift
Your hands.
Your Lord is here.
He is in on all your plans.

All are welcome at Riverside Church.
None turned away with sorrow
Or hurt.
Bless our church, Lord, as we do your
Will.
Praise God. Give glory.
Our God is real.

A Special Doctor

Some doctors here may come and go
Without much mention,
Without much show.

But you, my friend, will be a different case,
Because you worked
At a caring pace.

The patients will miss your personal
Touch.
We've all appreciated it so very much.

The staff will miss that extra mile
You seem to go and still maintain
A smile.

I myself have learned from you
A patient's importance,
Whether they are old or new.

A heart like yours is sincerely true,
Making it impossible
To ever replace you.

Beverly

I sure do love Beverly. She was
Special to me.
I know she is in heaven looking
Down on you and me.

She never did spank me, but she
Did Lela and Butch.
She had to make sure they did
As told and such.

George was in charge, you could
Plainly see.
But I always liked the way Beverly
Treated me.

She was a stay-at-home mom, and her
Family came first.
Devoted to them all,
She would often of them boast.

We often talked of the Bible,
God,
Things and people,
What it's like up above.

One more has been plucked from
Our family on earth
But will be waiting for us
In that heavenly church.

A close family is a blessing—the
Bible tells us so—
But it sure is hard when we
Have to let go.

A Job Well Done

To have a son so many loved.
He wore a smile every day.
Such a sweet nature, so good
With his kids.
"You must be proud," I would
Say

He never cussed. He did not
Drink. Never drove fast or
Mean.
"You must be proud," I say again,
"To have been parents of Lee."

He wasn't a saint—none of us
Are—but he came close. To this
I have heard.
He went to church, had a
Good heart. Helping others
Wherever he turned.

No parents are perfect. We all
Know that as we try our best
With our kids.

They can try our souls and
Break our hearts, but that's all
Normal, I'm told.

I'm thinking you must have
Done something right when
Raising your little boy.

He was a joy while here and
Touched so many hearts.
This would not have been
If you had not done your part.

Loving Mother

It's hard to give up a loving mother,
Especially one that has always been there
For you.

A mother is there to pick you up and has
Always gotten you through.

But Bod has told us from the start
Our lives will not last long.

We all know it never seems real, so
We are shocked when he takes
One home.

A lucky person, you have been,
To have had a caring mother
Since birth.

She did her living while on this earth,
To help make you what you are
Worth.

God has another job for her now.
He trained her well while she
Was here.

He must have needed her and missed her much,
To call her home in such a rush.

Just be grateful for her love that you
Had for these years.
Maybe that will sooth your heart
While shedding tears.

Now live your life and give
To your children
That love and attention
That you had.

So when you are gone and
They think of you,
They will smile even though
They will be sad too.

Thoughts of Easter

When you think of Easter, what comes to your mind? Is it the Easter egg hunt and laughter of children searching intensely for hidden eggs in the grass? Hoping to find that prized egg? Your thoughts might center more on the new clothes, changing from old, drab, winter colors to the brighter pastels we feel so fresh in. Children parading in their patent leather shoes and hats with streamers. Little boys in suits with vests dressed like little men. Shiny shoes, hair combed down (a whole new look for most little boys). These same boys usually have on blue jeans. They steal your heart either way.

Songs that stir one's heart and bring back the past are "Easter Bonnet" and "Easter Parade." "Here Comes Peter Cotton Tail" was always a favorite. Easter also gives us an excuse for getting the entire family together for a special family dinner, complete with egg hunt.

Underneath all this is the true meaning of Easter. The cross on Calvary and the sad story of our precious Savior shedding his blood for us and the tears shed that day. And the hope and happiness that broke out when he rose from the dead—a new beginning. He had told the disciples all along he would return from the dead, but they still did not realize his plan.

I hope this Easter season brings hope to you this year. A new beginning, enjoy your families and friends and celebrate Christ's resurrection. Be excited because he tells us he is coming again one day.

Born in a Stable

Baby Jesus was born that night
In Bethlehem, they say.

May and Joseph stayed in a stable,
And in a manger, he lay.

A star above marked the spot
Of the birth. He lay his head
On hay.

God sent his son to earth that day.
For our sins, he would pay

Praise God for that blessed time.
Praise God for that Savior
Of yours and mine.

Uncle George

To write a poem
About George Dunn
Is not an easy task.

You can find many folks
Who agree with me.
All you have to do is ask.

He would get a kick
Out of embarrassing you
Or really getting your goat.

To remember his laugh,
His sparkling eyes.
It's a memory I remember most.

He was proud of family
Right from the start.
If you knew George,
You know he had a soft heart.

He invited people to
Thanksgiving Day.
None of us really knew them,
But what the hey!

When he was a cop,
He once pulled over my bus.
All this to make quite a fuss.

He asked for me like
I committed a crime.
Things like this he did
All the time.

On my wedding day,
He sent me a card—
Instead of good wishes,
A sympathy card!

A laugh a minute, he
Lived for the day.
When it comes to George,
There's so much to say.

He is happier now
Than he has ever been.
I'm so glad that
We all knew him.

A wittiness and a way
With others,
He was so close
To his sisters and brothers.

We don't have to worry
About George any more.
He has completed what
We all were born for.

Aunt Mary

My aunt Mary
Is so dear to me.

Her house was like home to me.
I loved her crazy place.

Down there, kids were
Everywhere.
They seemed always in your face.

Mary meant business.
You better mind.
If you didn't,
She would blister your behind!

She has always been
Good to me.
Shared lots of smiles,
Not even really mean.

All the memories
Of Mary in my heart
Will never leave me.
She's been there from the start.

Vacations together, visits
To the lake.
Laughs and giggles are
Truly not fake.

So, forever in my heart,
She remains special.
Even after this life ends,
I know she is always
My friend.

Christian Ladies

Someone may need you.
You do not know
Someone who has a way.
Problems do not show.

Paying attention goes a
Long way
To sense when your
Brother is in
A bad way.

A smile, a kind word
Opens a line so
People's problems are
Heard and we're not blind.

Pray each day God
Will make you aware
Of those in need
To show we care.

Join me, ladies, as
Onward we go.
His will be done,
And our love
Will show.

Christian ladies are
Called by the Lord
To do his work in love,
Not with a sword.

Open your ears
To each one in need.
Let us start the way
By planting a seed.

Welcome

Welcome, each one, to
Our banquet this year.
Hoping to bring you a
Smile and good cheer.

Our ladies' group is special,
And we wish you
The best.
So come on and join our
Meetings and mingle with
The rest.

Decorations are shining,
And love around.
Praise God for coming.
Enjoy all the blessings
You've found.

Share a few laughs
And share a few smiles.
Share enough love
To last you awhile.

Mother of Love

My mother is a very special lady to all.
A heart of gold she has,
For young and old.

She will always go that extra mile.
Her trademark is
A genuine smile.

Children love her right from the start.
They seem to sense her
Caring heart.

Older people flock to her side.
She will be their friend and is glad
To be their guide.

Sometimes I am jealous she shares
All this love,
Doing so much for so many,
But well done.

What a blessing I was given
From above to have such a wonderful
Mother of love.

Angels Are among Us

Angels are among us,
I truly believe.
One to comfort and watch
While life happens to me.

God knew I would need one
Right from the start,
So he assigned me a good
One to do his part.

I truly don't know what an
Angel's job means,
But I know they help me.
It truly does seem.

I don't know if they have
Halos and harps,
Wings or Barefoot or
All the other parts.

But this I know from
Side,
Angels are sent
At just the right time.

God's Word tells me they really
Are there.
This shows me that God
Really cares.

I have felt a comfort
During hard times for me.
So, pray for your angel,
And then you will see.

A Special Church

Every church has its own special way
That the members yearn for,
And they need to come and pray.

Ours is no different; we're one like the rest.
More love than some, and the people are the best.

We have special singings and dinners a must.
Most people here never really fuss.

We pray for each other sincerely and true,
And if you let us know, we all will pray for you.

When we all get to heaven, we will sing and shout.
Until then, we'll work here.
That's what it is all about.

We are all on the Lord's side. It is definitely true.
If you come to our church,
You will feel it too.

Blessings abounding are here for the taking.
Get yours and help others.
There are more blessings
In the making.

This poem is a tribute to each one of you,
The caring and sharing I've
Received here too.

You have all made a difference in my life.
It is true.
I pray I may pass this on to someone too.

Thankful Heart

We all say we are thankful for all we have and what God has done for us. And we really are to a large degree, but do we truly act like it? Read this short story. It was written to show that a kindness can go a long way, but as I read it, I felt there was more to the big picture. See what you think.

As women, we become overwhelmed from our roles. We are the comforter, the cook, the nurse, the chauffeur, the teacher—sometimes I'm the electrician, plumber, the preacher. It's almost too much! Who put me in charge of all this? Me—poor, pitiful me. I truly am thankful to be given the opportunity to do all these things, but I sure can wallow in self-pity plenty of times.

What is your hope built on?

Jeremiah 17:7: blessed is the man that trusts in the Lord and whose hope the Lord is.

A lot of us try to handle our problems ourselves till it is so obvious we need to call on the Lord. We finally do. But why do we do that? We are Christians, we proclaim. We rely on the Lord, but talking about it and doing it are two different things. He is there for us no matter how small it is.

He heals sometimes. Sometimes it is not his plan, but he does heal. Some people debate with you regarding this. You believe your way. I'll believe my way, and all the time, God is answering prayers.

We never know where life will take us. What circumstances we might end up in—living a long life or a short life. We don't know, but God knows. We need to live one day at a time and do all we can for God in whatever length of time we have. But we seem to live life like it will be this way forever.

Remember the *Titanic*? We never know. God is in control. We think it is crazy, but God is in control.

I was thinking on my way to work about everything I needed to do when I got off today. Run here, run there. We all do this, and you have to make plans.

How quickly I could be gone, and you for that matter. Then all my plans wouldn't matter. Everything we get so wound up about would still be here—but not us. We would be with our Lord. Your clothes are here, your car. But not your body and spirit. We forget to make the most of today, planning for tomorrow.

We need to live for today, praying, reading our Bible, and getting ourselves right with God so we can do what God would have us do, not waste the time he has given us.

This little devotional is for me as well as you. Sometimes when I go to my Dad's, I think, *Where is Mother? Her stuff is here but not her.* The stuff doesn't matter. It is our spirit. Show love and kindness. Be patient with others. Go out of your way to be more like God.

I'm going to make a true effort to be more like I should be. We are in such a rush we don't have time for people.

What if you do not pursue your calling? Have you ever heard "God will take care of you"? He will and does. You know, I wonder how many times I could have been harmed physically or emotionally that he took care of me and I did not even know it?

Read the poem "Footprints in the Sand."

Make the Most of Your Life

How many of you have thought if your circumstances were just better, you would be a better person? I have an old devotional book edited by A. J. Russell, an author only referred to as Barbour Publishing. Let me share.

Many times, I thought that if I had a better house, I could have people to my house and witness more. More Bible studies. I just know I could do more of God's will if my house was not almost one hundred years old. But God says to change me, not my house. He'll take care of all that. Change me—never look back. Look for his guidance today. I could miss his blessings today while I'm worrying over tomorrow.

Faith is a little big word. Where is our faith? Look at Mark 4:40.

We have heard this verse from Matthew 6:30 many times. If we have faith in God, why are we so worried? If you have made mistakes in the past, just move on and ask for God's help.

We all have done things, said things, and thought things we did not mean. Look to God. He will restore our ways.

We all know the children's song "The Wise Man Built His House upon a Rock." We need to build our faith on the rock, not the sand. When we were studying Revelations, lots of scary information, but why worry? Christians will be taken care of. We need to get our job done to spread the warning.

All we have to do is look to God. Seek him and have faith. He'll do the rest.

Psalms 54. Do you lose your temper? I have gotten mad and thrown a salt shaker. As soon as I did, I thought, *Now who's gonna clean that up?* I drove off then and thought, *Now I have to go back.* I bet you've done things like this. If not, I'm ashamed I did. I haven't always been perfect.

God's plan is the right plan. Have faith and talk to him often about his plans for you.

Today I was needing to talk to my mother. I closed my eyes. I told the Lord she wasn't just my mother but my friend. I had some things I needed to talk to her about. I miss her. I haven't got that friend. I told her everything good and bad. Then it came to me from God. "I am your friend—naturally." I thought, *Well I know that, but I mean a mother friend.* "I am your mother friend, your true friend, master of the universe." So I thought of a song the choir practiced last night, "Majesty." I thought, *What a magnificent God—all powerful.*

So I told the Lord all the things in my mind. He touched me. I felt peace. I really do still have my true friend. I can tell him anything everything, not just going through space, the motions, but results are given.

God's love is pure, no backstabbing. Humans are made to tell you really quickly what *they* would do, but it might not be what *you* should do.

God's love is something we should strive for.

Pass the love around …

God intends all to have it. You know who my best friends are—you ladies.

You've heard *a friend in need is a friend indeed*. Prove it to your friends, to your church, to your neighbors.

Let us strive to be there for each other. I truly almost called one of you (I won't say who). I would have asked, "Will you be like my mother so I can ask your opinion?" But I didn't have to. God stepped in and took care of it.

Be a Good Listener

I have read jokes, made light of different things at times. But I do want to be serious when I ask, Are you a good listener? This is an important quality for a Christian.

We are in such a hurry to get on with it. I remember going to my grandmother's on Sunday and listening to the older people talk. The majority of kids don't do that now. We can blame it on the kids. I get mad when they use their phones, iPad, or whatever and waste precious bonding opportunities. Many of us look them in the face and listen. I've noticed if I drill my granddaughter, she gives me short answers, but if I listen, she opens up. As we get older, we find it harder to listen because we know everything or we think we do. We don't listen as much as we give advice. We know what everyone should do and when.

I want to be a better listener. I know God wants me to be. He tells me so in John 8:43 and Proverbs 1:33.

I was stunned at what someone said to me. I knew she was having problems, and I said, "Let me know if you need someone to talk to." She replied, "Why, Linda, you don't have time to listen to my problems. You're way too busy." Oh man, you could have knocked me over. I am so ashamed. I thought I was a good Christian, but I was so caught up in activities I had forgotten my friend, and she was right. I was supposed to be God's helper. I failed. I was involved in my problems to the point I was obviously too busy! Later, when this friend broke her leg, I made a point to be there for her. I hope this helped me to look better as a Christian. We are all self-consumed. Are we listening to God? Is he nudging us? Are we too busy? Be a good listener to God, church, family, coworkers, friends, and the hurting.

Does all this shame you like it did me? I've tried to be a better listener. With prayer, we can be better Christians. Don't be concerned only about yourself and drop the ball with others. Someone may be trying to get your attention.

Happy Are the Generous

James 1:17.

Have you ever given someone a gift and gone out of your way to make it special—just to have them toss it aside, showing very little appreciation? It makes you feel like, *Why did I bother?* You may even have made sacrifices to see that the gift was obtained. But it meant nothing. I've had this again and again. I don't really think they even thought much about it. Nothing was done on purpose; most things aren't. They just don't know any better.

Do you know how to accept a gift graciously? I hope so. Think about how you have accepted gifts in the past.

You know God has given all of us gifts, and we've tossed them to the side without a thought or thank you. Sometimes we don't even open the gift. Isn't that crazy? That the Lord would give a gift and we wouldn't open it. But it's true.

We need to search our lives. Pray the Lord will show you your gifts so you may use them for him. You may be a good listener, singer, craft maker, cook. We are not all performers. Look deeper. You may brighten others' day with a smile. In 1 Corinthians 7:7 and James 1:17, there it is proof from God you indeed have a gift of your very own. Open it up. Accept it with love and use it to the fullness. Share your gift with others. Praise your Lord for this gift from him.

What Are Your Boundaries?

One day, God looked down at earth and saw outrageous, bad choices and sent an angel to check it out. The angel reported 95 percent were behaving badly, 5 percent were good. God was not pleased. So, he emailed the 5 percent and commended them for their choices. Do you know what it said? Just wondering. I didn't get it either.

God gives us a choice. He could have kept Adam and Eve from eating the fruit but gave them a choice.

Real freedom. We chose to crawl under the canopy created by God's love and live within his protection. He says, "Come unto me and I will give you rest" (Matthew 11:28).

Chocolate Story

A friend of Luci Swindoll's, Paul, received a shipment of chocolate. He did not deserve this. Did not earn it. Given to him free, no strings. Accepting God's gifts sets us free.

God has given each one of us a truckload of freedom through grace, all paid for by our Savior, Jesus Christ. We did not expect it. Did not earn it. Did not deserve it and cannot return it. So why don't we just receive it and enjoy it?

Mark 3:9–10. Jesus's example. Jesus got into a boat to get away from the pressing crowd. He did this not to escape their need but to preserve himself. He knew his earthly body needed protection from the pressure and prodding of those anxious people, so he spoke to them from a boat.

By reading Mark, we can perceive that his actions were saying no for him. Being separated, the crowd could not touch him. Was Jesus being selfish? Hardly. His behavior is an example of self-preservation. Sometimes the word is not necessary for our well-being.

Wedding vows.

A. Two people agree to be faithful and share boundaries.
B. When this is violated, consequences may result.

This is not meant to say you are to get out of all your responsibilities—just that you have choices.

But, for instance, let's name our character Miss Susie. She arranged the ladies' trip for Women of Faith the year before, seventy-five ladies. She arranged the rooms, transportation. It was located hours from home, and she had to arrange tickets and busing. An enormous job.

When they asked her to do it again, she firmly said no. That she plans to sit back and enjoy this year without so much responsibility and pressure. Is this selfish? No. Because by taking a break, someone else may have an opportunity to do it, and she may be anxious to do it the next year.

In Miss Susie's case, she serves the needs of her church and just needed a break. But doesn't the Bible say to love as Jesus loves and to serve others in love as he did? That does not mean that we do not take time for ourselves.

Just for instance, if a husband is abusive, a wife has to refuse to allow the behavior to continue, and if not, take the children and leave. Boundaries must be stated clearly and be understood. Imagine a child wants a brownie before supper in ten minutes, and her mom says no. If the child sneaks the brownie, running away and cramming it in her mouth, if the mom ignores this, the child is confused. Right and wrong may be negotiated. Some people do not have the ability to say no. Without feeling guilty, they figure the best way to get along is to be agreeable.

You cannot agree with everyone all the time and be doing God's will.

This does not encourage you to be a thorn in everyone's side by disagreeing so you can be heard.

In closing, pray for each other and yourselves that you may look at your life, set your priorities, and go to God to set these priorities.

Closing prayer, the Lord's Prayer.

Is Life Fair?

Do you ever feel like the world is not fair? Guess what? It's not. But God is always fair. When that other person gets that job? When you try your best just to get criticized? How about when you say something and someone gets mad when you only meant good? So many situations when the bad guy comes out on top.

Of course, we all have experienced this. How about the people that are even worse off than us?

What about the prodigal son? Remember the story we all know so well. Father with two sons, one shows no respect and leaves with his part of his father's estate while the father is still alive. He is living the life until his money runs out. Then he becomes aware his father's servants eat better than he does. So he comes home. His father has looked for him day in and day out.

He returns. Meanwhile, the other son has played it by the book. He was disgusted with his brother. Then as he approaches home, hearing party sounds at first, he was stunned. Then it turns to rage. How could his father do this? Father is welcoming his son back! Nothing makes sense. Grace should be the thing that unites us, but more often than not, it divides us. We weigh people's actions on human scales, but to God, those scales don't work.

Tex Watson had no roots, no belief, went to California for peace and love. He met up with Charles Manson and became part of his murderous clan. After being convicted, he is now in prison. He was saved in 1975 by an evangelist in prison. In 1983, he was ordained a minister. Still in prison, thirty-five years later, he walks the prison yard bringing God's Word.

God knows no boundaries. He goes to prison yards, cancer wards, and school yards. If we tried to write about all this, we would run out of ink.

Fair?

Discuss with your group or think about this.

Are We Judging?

Luke 33–37.

In these verses, the Lord has told us specifically we are not to judge others. Sometimes this is hard to do. We are humans, but with God's help, we can do this when his spirit lives in us. You are capable of things even you don't know you are capable of. Has someone done or said something to you? You just can't forgive. Pray about it. God will take this from you. You won't have to do it. God will do it for you. How many of us (no show of hands please) have looked how another lady is dressed and said or even thought, *Did she really look in the mirror and say "Wow, this looks great!"?* It may be she is revealing too much cleavage, or it's too tight or even too big, or it doesn't match. In reality and God's way, why should we care? Church especially is not a place to judge someone. A no-no. A real no-no. Be glad they are here. They may not be back.

There is no room in a Christian heart for hatred toward your enemies. God has forgiven our dirty sins. Forgive others. Why do we deserve to be forgiven?

Give and it will be given to you. Example: my mom and dad spent their lives helping everyone. Now people have helped them three-fold. Most in the room have experienced this at one time or another.

Luke 6:27

He tells us to listen, love your enemies, do good to those who hate you. Bless those who curse you, pray for those who mistreat you. Read those verses in Luke to yourselves.

We are a loving church, a loving and caring group of women who have to be careful to include each person. Each lady that visits or comes here is part of our group. No room for clicks in church. We are all in this together. God will bless you for it.

We all have friends we are closer to than others. But let's all make an effort to make everyone, especially ladies at our church, part of our group. God has chosen us to do a job here—to make this a sweet haven for all. To add that special touch of sweetness. Love one another; treat others like we want to be treated—these are not my words but God's words. John 15:12.

Our church is known for friendliness and charity and love. Let us band together to make God proud. Luke 1:37.

Do you hear me? Read again. We can fill this church; we can fill this room; we can fill our children and teens. Read again Luke 1:37. Do you believe in God? Do you believe his Word? We need to pray more—read his Word more.

If you are concerned that things need to be changed in your church and your family, you need to pray and read your Bible. Ask the Lord and do all you can with his guidance to make it happen. God made us promises in the Bible. Now let us do our part.

To Know the Love of Christ

Key Verses   Ephesians 3:16–21

Think a moment. What in your own life shows you that God loves you no matter what? Put some real thinking power into this. If you are a Christian, it won't take you long before you can give an answer. Tough times come to each of us. Everyone in this room has experienced hard times, and some of us are at this time experiencing difficulties. Sometimes we know our friends are having problems and pray for them. But we need to attend to their pain. Love our brothers and sisters. Go that extra mile. This is the Lord's order for us as Christians. We are his soldiers. We are all capable of kindness.

1. Can you smile?
2. Can you give a kind word?
3. Can you offer a ride if needed?
4. Can you pick up a phone?
5. Can you drop by the hospital?

Lots of simple things can make a big difference. But life gets in the way. I am guilty too! Life gets in the way. Who give us life?

Our God can work wonders through us. While we are talking about problems, let us remember how we feel when we don't have a ride to work or need a smile from someone or just a kind word.

Quit wasting time. Now is the time.

Ladies: we have a mission. We are up for the job. Love one another.

Closing devotional with one verse of "Onward Christian Soldiers."

Printed in the United States
By Bookmasters